This book Belongs To:

____

Coloring Book For Kids
2-4 years

LEARN AND COLOR THE ANIMALS

30 drawings to color

Camel

Cat

Bee

Butterfly

Caterpillar

chick

Crab

Crocodile

Dolphin

Dog

Duck

Fish

Fox

Frog

Giraffe

Horse

Lion

Mermaid

Monkey

Octopus

Rabbit

Rooster

Shark

Sheep

Snail

Snake

Tiger

Turtle

Unicorn

Wolf